THE BOMBING OF PEARL HARBOR

GRAPHIC HISTORIES

STORY:
ELIZABETH HUDSON-GOFF AND MICHAEL V. USCHAN

ILLUSTRATIONS:
GUUS FLOOR, MIKE BEAR, ALEX CAMPBELL, AND ANTHONY SPAY

WORLD ALMANAC® LIBRARY

REMEMBER PEARL HARBOR!

EARLY IN THE MORNING OF DECEMBER 7, 1941, DEATH RAINED FROM THE SKIES OVER HAWAII. HUNDREDS OF JAPANESE PLANES BOMBED A U.S. MILITARY BASE CALLED PEARL HARBOR. FOR OVER AN HOUR, BOMBS EXPLODED! U.S. PLANES ON THE GROUND AND BATTLESHIPS WERE DESTROYED! THIS SURPRISE ATTACK FORCED THE UNITED STATES INTO WORLD WAR II, A CONFLICT THAT HAD BEGUN IN EUROPE IN 1939 AND SOON SPREAD TO ASIA AND AFRICA.

BY 1941, MILLIONS OF PEOPLE HAD ALREADY DIED BECAUSE OF THE FIGHTING AND OTHER HORRORS OF THE WAR. UNTIL THE AWFUL EVENTS AT PEARL HARBOR, THE UNITED STATES HAD STAYED OUT OF WAR. BUT ON THAT FATEFUL DAY, EVERYTHING CHANGED.

MANY WARS BEGIN BECAUSE CERTAIN NATIONS WANT TO GAIN POWER OVER OTHER NATIONS. IN EUROPE, NAZI GERMANY THREATENED TO TAKE OVER THE ENTIRE CONTINENT.

JAPAN WANTED TO RULE OVER ASIA. JAPANESE SOLDIERS SWARMED INTO SEVERAL COUNTRIES, READY TO FIGHT!

GERMANY, JAPAN, ITALY, AND A FEW OTHER NATIONS JOINED TOGETHER, FORMING THE AXIS POWERS.

BUT MANY COUNTRIES WERE TRYING TO FIGHT BACK AGAINST THE AXIS. THEY WERE CALLED THE ALLIES. THE ALLIES INCLUDED GREAT BRITAIN, FRANCE, RUSSIA, AUSTRALIA, AND CHINA, AMONG OTHERS. THE ALLIES WERE STRONG, AND DETERMINED TO WIN. BUT THE AXIS POWERS WERE ALSO POWERFUL.

ADOLF HITLER, GERMANY'S LEADER, WANTED POWER OVER ALL OF EUROPE. EVEN BEFORE THE ATTACK ON PEARL HARBOR, GERMANY HAD ALREADY SEIZED CONTROL OF SOME EUROPEAN COUNTRIES.

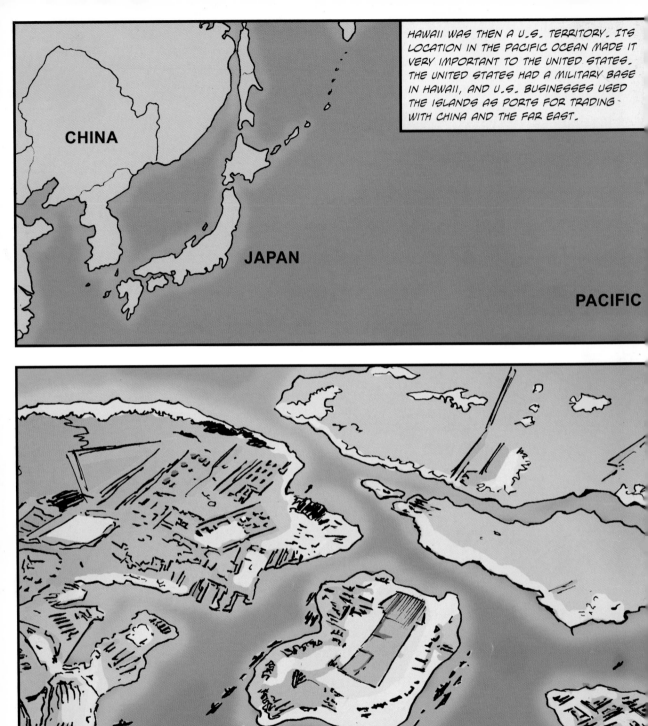

HAWAII WAS THEN A U.S. TERRITORY. ITS LOCATION IN THE PACIFIC OCEAN MADE IT VERY IMPORTANT TO THE UNITED STATES. THE UNITED STATES HAD A MILITARY BASE IN HAWAII, AND U.S. BUSINESSES USED THE ISLANDS AS PORTS FOR TRADING WITH CHINA AND THE FAR EAST.

CHINA

JAPAN

PACIFIC

IN 1940, U.S. PRESIDENT FRANKLIN D. ROOSEVELT MOVED THE U.S. NAVY'S PACIFIC FLEET FROM CALIFORNIA TO HAWAII. ITS HEADQUARTERS—PEARL HARBOR ON THE ISLAND OF OAHU.

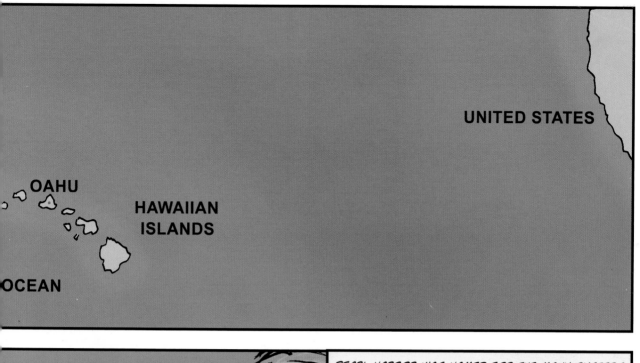

UNITED STATES

OAHU

HAWAIIAN
ISLANDS

OCEAN

PEARL HARBOR WAS NAMED FOR THE MANY OYSTERS
FOUND IN ITS WATERS AND FOR THEIR PRECIOUS
PEARLS. THE HARBOR WAS A PEACEFUL PARADISE.
ONLY THE PRESENCE OF WARSHIPS HINTED AT THE
SERIOUS MILITARY DUTIES GOING ON THERE.

THE NAVAL BASE IS A DAGGER BEING POINTED AT OUR THROATS!

THE JAPANESE WERE WORRIED ABOUT THE U.S. SHIPS STATIONED AT PEARL HARBOR.

DANGER BEGAN TO GROW BY THE DAY . . .

IN 1941, PRESIDENT ROOSEVELT ORDERED AMERICANS TO STOP SELLING WAR SUPPLIES LIKE STEEL AND OIL TO JAPAN. THIS ANGERED THE JAPANESE.

IN OCTOBER, GENERAL HIDEKI TOJO BECAME JAPAN'S PRIME MINISTER. HE DECIDED TO ATTACK THE UNITED STATES. HIS PLAN—TO SINK THE U.S. NAVY'S ENTIRE PACIFIC FLEET AT PEARL HARBOR.

JAPANESE DIPLOMATS WENT TO WASHINGTON, D.C., TO TALK WITH U.S. OFFICIALS.

THEY PRETENDED TO BE INTERESTED IN PEACE. IN FACT, THEY WERE PLANNING A SURPRISE ATTACK. THEY WERE GOING TO DESTROY "THE DAGGER."

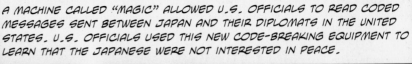
A MACHINE CALLED "MAGIC" ALLOWED U.S. OFFICIALS TO READ CODED MESSAGES SENT BETWEEN JAPAN AND THEIR DIPLOMATS IN THE UNITED STATES. U.S. OFFICIALS USED THIS NEW CODE-BREAKING EQUIPMENT TO LEARN THAT THE JAPANESE WERE NOT INTERESTED IN PEACE.

THIS DISPATCH IS TO BE CONSIDERED A WAR WARNING . . . AN AGGRESSIVE MOVE BY JAPAN IS EXPECTED WITHIN THE NEXT FEW DAYS

NO ADMITTANCE TOP SECRET

IN LATE NOVEMBER 1941, U.S. OFFICIALS REALIZED THAT SOMETHING HORRIBLE WAS ABOUT TO HAPPEN. THEY ISSUED A "WAR WARNING" TO THE U.S. NAVY AND ARMY IN THE PACIFIC.

IN HAWAII, THE WARNINGS WENT TO ADMIRAL HUSBAND E. KIMMEL, COMMANDER OF THE PACIFIC FLEET. THEY ALSO WENT TO LIEUTENANT GENERAL WALTER SHORT, WHO COMMANDED THE SOLDIERS THERE.

TIME WAS CLEARLY RUNNING OUT. BUT STILL NO ONE KNEW WHEN OR HOW THE ATTACK WOULD HAPPEN.

ON NOVEMBER 26, 1941, THE JAPANESE BEGAN THEIR JOURNEY. THIRTY-THREE SHIPS CALLED AIRCRAFT CARRIERS BROUGHT WARPLANES CLOSER TO HAWAII.

THE SHIPS WAITED 220 MILES (350 KILOMETERS) NORTH OF OAHU. THE WARPLANE PILOTS WERE TOLD TO WAIT UNTIL THEY WERE ORDERED TO ATTACK.

THE U.S. NAVY WAS NOT ON ALERT ON DECEMBER 7, 1941. TO THEM IT WAS JUST ANOTHER DAY.

BEFORE DAWN THAT SAME DAY, JAPANESE PILOTS PREPARED FOR THEIR MISSION. THEN 183 JAPANESE WARPLANES TOOK OFF.

A SECOND GROUP OF 167 WAR PLANES SOON FOLLOWED.

AHEAD AND FAR BELOW THEY WOULD FIND THEIR TARGET—PEARL HARBOR.

AT 7:52 A.M., THE FIRST PLANES ROARED OVER OAHU.

"TORA! TORA! TORA!" RADIOED THE ATTACK COMMANDER BACK TO HIS ADMIRAL. "TORA" ("TIGER") WAS THE CODE WORD SIGNALING THAT THE JAPANESE HAD SURPRISED THE ENEMY.

"IT WAS LIKE THE SKY WAS FILLED WITH FIREFLIES."

—JAPANESE BOMBER PILOT ABE ZENJII

THE JAPANESE PILOTS COULD SEE THE CROOKED SHAPE OF THE TARGET BELOW. IN THE NEW MORNING SUN, THEY COULD SEE THE DARK SHAPES OF THE U.S. WARSHIPS ANCHORED IN THE PEACEFUL HARBOR.

AS THE JAPANESE WERE MAKING THEIR APPROACH, THE AMERICANS WERE GOING ABOUT THEIR NORMAL MORNING ROUTINES. SOME NAVY MEN WERE CLEANING SHIP DECKS. SOME PEOPLE WERE EATING BREAKFAST. SOME NEARBY FAMILIES WERE GETTING READY TO GO TO CHURCH.

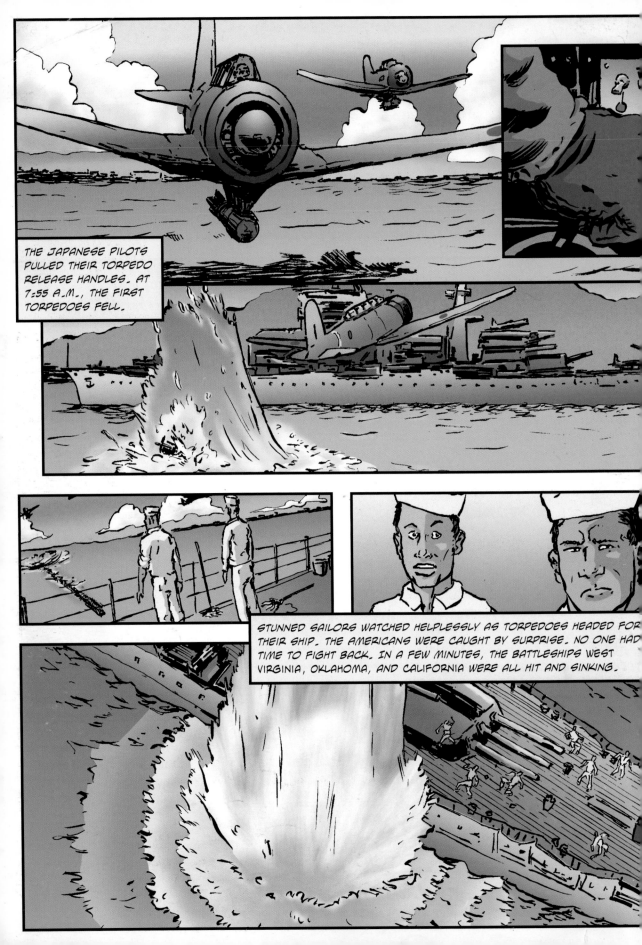

THE JAPANESE PILOTS PULLED THEIR TORPEDO RELEASE HANDLES. AT 7:55 A.M., THE FIRST TORPEDOES FELL.

STUNNED SAILORS WATCHED HELPLESSLY AS TORPEDOES HEADED FOR THEIR SHIP. THE AMERICANS WERE CAUGHT BY SURPRISE. NO ONE HAD TIME TO FIGHT BACK. IN A FEW MINUTES, THE BATTLESHIPS WEST VIRGINIA, OKLAHOMA, AND CALIFORNIA WERE ALL HIT AND SINKING.

SUDDENLY THE AIR EXPLODED WITH TERRIBLE SHRIEKS AND BLASTS FROM THE BOMBER PLANES. THEY WERE EVERYWHERE. THERE WAS NO PLACE TO HIDE.

A HUGE BOMB HIT THE DECK OF THE ARIZONA. IT SET OFF AN EXPLOSION THAT SENT A FIREBALL SOARING HIGH INTO THE AIR.

IN ONLY 9 MINUTES, THE GREAT SHIP SANK. NEARLY HALF THE AMERICANS KILLED THAT DAY WERE ON THE ARIZONA.

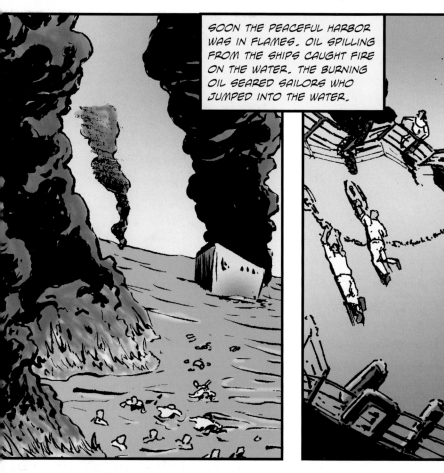

SOON THE PEACEFUL HARBOR WAS IN FLAMES. OIL SPILLING FROM THE SHIPS CAUGHT FIRE ON THE WATER. THE BURNING OIL SEARED SAILORS WHO JUMPED INTO THE WATER.

SAILORS PRIED OPEN DOORS TO HELP TRAPPED MEN. SCREAMS OF PAIN FROM THE SEA MIXED WITH THE ROAR OF PLANES IN THE AIR.

POOM

As the bombs fell, sailors on board ships rushed to their battle stations. They fired machine guns and antiaircraft guns.

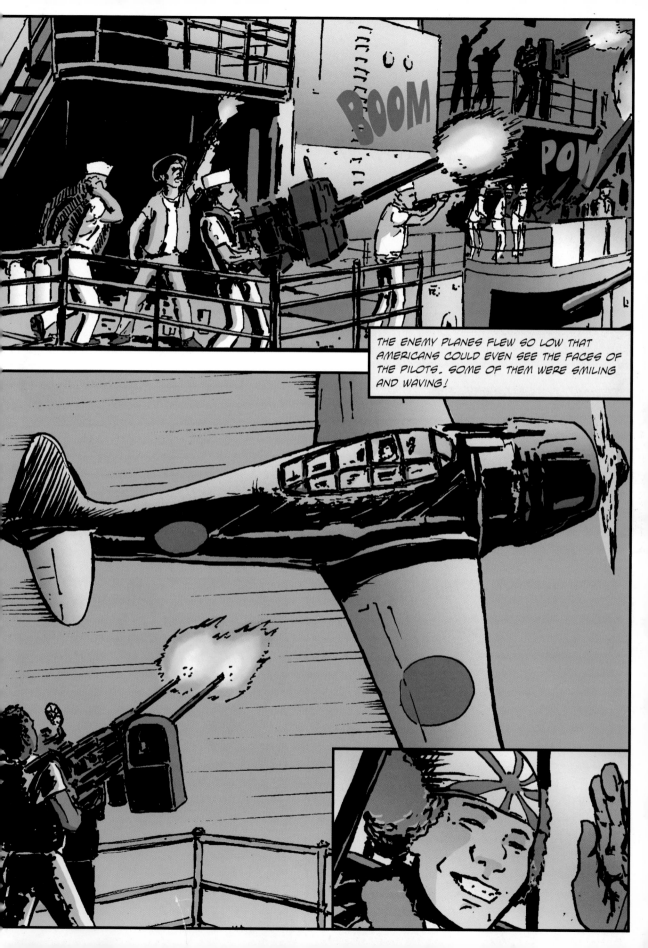

THE ENEMY PLANES FLEW SO LOW THAT AMERICANS COULD EVEN SEE THE FACES OF THE PILOTS. SOME OF THEM WERE SMILING AND WAVING!

PEARL HARBOR WAS THE MAIN TARGET, BUT JAPANESE PLANES STRUCK THE OAHU AIRFIELDS, TOO. THEIR GOAL WAS TO DESTROY U.S. PLANES.

ONLY 14 U.S. PILOTS GOT INTO THE AIR TO FIGHT BACK.

RESCUERS TRIED TO SAVE SAILORS TRAPPED IN OVERTURNED SHIPS. THEY PULLED SOME TO SAFETY, BUT SADLY, MANY SAILORS DIED BEFORE THEY COULD BE REACHED.

THE HOSPITALS FILLED UP WITH INJURED PEOPLE. THERE WERE NOT ENOUGH ROOMS FOR ALL THE WOUNDED.

PEARL HARBOR NAVAL HOSPITAL

IN THE ATTACK ON PEARL HARBOR, 2,340 SOLDIERS AND SAILORS WERE KILLED. OVER 1,000 PEOPLE WERE WOUNDED; SOME WERE DISABLED FOR THE REST OF THEIR LIVES. FORTY-EIGHT CIVILIANS DIED, AND THIRTY-FIVE WERE INJURED.

PEARL HARBOR WAS A NIGHTMARE FOR THE U.S. NAVY. TWENTY-ONE SHIPS SUNK OR DAMAGED, AND 164 PLANES DESTROYED. THE NAVY WORKED QUICKLY TO BECOME STRONG AGAIN. IT REPAIRED ITS FLEET. IT RAISED SUNKEN SHIPS. WITHIN A FEW MONTHS, PEARL HARBOR WAS READY FOR WAR.

YESTERDAY, DECEMBER 7, 1941—A DATE WHICH WILL LIVE IN INFAMY...

ON DECEMBER 8, PRESIDENT FRANKLIN D. ROOSEVELT CONVINCED CONGRESS TO DECLARE WAR AGAINST JAPAN.

GERMANY AND ITALY THEN DECLARED WAR ON THE UNITED STATES. THE UNITED STATES HAD NOW ENTERED WORLD WAR II.

OVER THE NEXT THREE YEARS, THE ALLIES CONTINUED TO FIGHT IN WORLD WAR II. GERMANY SURRENDERED IN MAY 1945, ENDING WORLD WAR II IN EUROPE. BUT JAPAN CONTINUED TO FIGHT. PRESIDENT ROOSEVELT HAD DIED IN APRIL 1945, AND THE NEW U.S. PRESIDENT, HARRY S. TRUMAN, FACED A DIFFICULT DECISION— HOW TO GET JAPAN TO SURRENDER. IN AUGUST OF 1945, THE PRESIDENT GAVE THE ORDER TO DROP TWO ATOMIC BOMBS—ONE ON HIROSHIMA AND ONE, A FEW DAYS LATER, ON NAGASAKI. ON AUGUST 14, 1945, JAPAN SURRENDERED.

AFTER MILLIONS OF DEATHS AROUND THE WORLD, WORLD WAR II WAS FINALLY OVER.

IN 1962, A MEMORIAL WAS OPENED IN PEARL HARBOR. IT RESTS ACROSS THE DECK OF THE SUNKEN BATTLESHIP ARIZONA. THE MEMORIAL CONTAINS THE NAMES OF THE THOUSANDS OF MEN AND WOMEN WHO WERE KILLED DURING THE ATTACK ON DECEMBER 7, 1941.

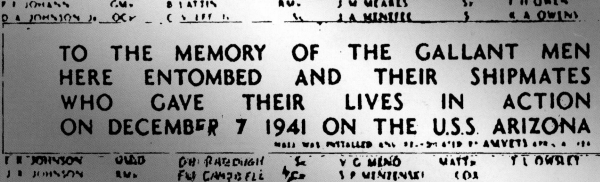

TO THE MEMORY OF THE GALLANT MEN HERE ENTOMBED AND THEIR SHIPMATES WHO GAVE THEIR LIVES IN ACTION ON DECEMBER 7 1941 ON THE U.S.S. ARIZONA

THE USS ARIZONA MEMORIAL IS A REMINDER OF THE JAPANESE ATTACK ON PEARL HARBOR. THE ATTACK WAS THE WORST EVER MADE AGAINST AMERICANS ON U.S. SOIL—UNTIL THE TERRORIST ATTACKS ON SEPTEMBER 11, 2001.

PEARL HARBOR IS STILL AN IMPORTANT MILITARY BASE. TODAY, IT IS HOME TO MORE THAN 81,000 MEMBERS OF THE MILITARY AND THEIR FAMILIES. IT IS A PEACEFUL, HAPPY COMMUNITY. FEW SIGNS REMAIN OF THAT TERRIBLE DAY IN 1941. BUT AMERICANS WILL ALWAYS "REMEMBER PEARL HARBOR."

MORE BOOKS TO READ

Air Raid—Pearl Harbor!: The Story of December 7, 1941.   Theodore Taylor
   (Harcourt Children's Books)
The Attack on Pearl Harbor: America Enters World War II. First Battles (series).
   Tim McNeese   (Morgan Reynolds Publishing)
The Bombing of Pearl Harbor. Landmark Events in American History (series).
   Michael V. Ushan (World Almanac Library)
Pearl Harbor. Checkerboard History Library (series). Tamara L. Britton
   (Checkerboard Books)
Remember Pearl Harbor: Japanese and American Survivors Tell Their Stories.
   Thomas B. Allen   (National Georgraphic Children's Books)

WEB SITES

Pearl Harbor Attacked
www.pearlharborattacked.com

Pearl Harbor Raid, 7 December 1941
www.history.navy.mil/photos/events/wwii-pac/pearlhbr/pearlhbr.htm

Remembering Pearl Harbor
plasma.nationalgeographic.com/pearlharbor

Road to Pearl Harbor
history.acusd.edu/gen/WW2Timeline/RD-PEARL.html

USS Arizona Memorial
www.nps.gov/usar

Please visit our web site at: **www.garethstevens.com**
For a free color catalog describing our list of high-quality books,
call 1-800-542-2595 (USA) or 1-800-387-3178 (Canada).

Library of Congress Cataloging-in-Publication Data

Hudson-Goff, Elizabeth.
    The bombing of Pearl Harbor / Elizabeth Hudson-Goff and Michael V. Uschan.
      p. cm. — (Graphic histories)
    Includes bibliographical references.
    ISBN-13: 978-0-8368-6206-5 (lib. bdg.)
    ISBN-10: 0-8368-6206-6 (lib. bdg.)
    ISBN-13: 978-0-8368-6258-4 (softcover)
    ISBN-10: 0-8368-6258-9 (softcover)
    1. Pearl Harbor (Hawaii), Attack on, 1941—Comic books, strips, etc.
  I. Uschan, Michael V., 1948- II. Title. III. Series.
  D767.92.G64   2006
  940.54'26693—dc22   2005027875

First published in 2006 by
World Almanac® Library
An imprint of Gareth Stevens Publishing
1 Reader's Digest Road
Pleasantville, NY 10570-7000 USA

Copyright © 2006 by World Almanac® Library.

Produced by Design Press, a division of the
Savannah College of Art and Design
Design: Janice Shay and Maria Angela Rojas
Editing: Kerri O'Hern and Elizabeth Hudson-Goff
Illustration: Layouts by Guus Floor, pencils by Mike Bear,
    inks by Alex Campbell, color by Anthony Spay
World Almanac® Library editorial direction: Mark Sachner
    and Valerie J. Weber
World Almanac® Library art direction: Tammy West

Printed in the United States of America

3 4 5 6 7 8 9 10 09 08 07